We Call So Many Feelings Love

poems by

SARA SEBASTIAN

Permission granted from the Andy Warhol Foundation for the Visual Arts, Inc. to use a quote in the poem, "Let There Be a Last Time".

Permission granted from John Sebastian to use one of his song titles in the poem, "Why Now?"

The poem, "Stream and Sun at Glendalough" by W.B. Yeats, was originally published in his book, The Winding Stair and Other Poems, by Macmillan and Co, London, in 1933.

Ordering Information:
Quantity sales. Special discounts are available on quantity purchases by corporations, associations, and others. For details, contact the author at the email address above.

Library of Congress Cataloging-in-Publication Data

Sebastian, Sara.
We Call So Many Feelings Love
LCCN 2023921141   ISBN 979-8-218-31326-5 (print)   ISBN 979-8-218-31356-2 (ebook)
POETRY / American / General
POETRY / Inspirational & Religious
POETRY / Women Authors

Place of publication: West Linn, Oregon

Cover photo by Dacia Pierson
Cover designed by the author

www.sarasebastian.co

We Call So Many Feelings Love/Sara Sebastian. —1st ed.
ISBN 9798218313265

For Leilani

Stream And Sun At Glendalough

Through intricate motions ran
Stream and gliding sun
And all my heart seemed gay:
Some stupid thing that I had done
Made my attention stray.

Repentance keeps my heart impure;
But what am I that dare
Fancy that I can
Better conduct myself or have more
Sense than a common man?

What motion of the sun or stream
Or eyelid shot the gleam
That pierced my body through?
What made me live like these that seem
Self-born, born anew?

—W. B. Yeats

CONTENTS

Part I: Desire

Constant

Will I be able
To let it be a beautiful moment
Not scarred by rejection
Or cursed by hope?

I messaged you on my parents' wedding anniversary
Even though they are divorced.
Hope still does
What courage gives it room to do.

This is confusing
For me also
Wanting
And wanting not to want
Wanting
And wanting not to want

The key difference is
I don't need your love
I want it
(And that makes all the difference)

How does desire make things real?
And is it tangible for only me?

Eating a Watermelon

I took a slice outside
The sun still bright and hot for 6 pm
The birds still out
The dog still right there
I said, "No"
In between my first few slurps
And he listened, giving me some space

I slowed my eating
Slowed my slurping
Pressed my lips into the flesh
Imprinted by my teeth
Is this why people love pressing their faces onto windows
To feel their eyelashes come up against
To have their cheeks held
To feel something on their lips
I held a green mouth to mine

The rind so thick
To hold something so juicy

What Does Curiosity Kill?

Maybe when my intuition spoke at the start
Clearly and calmly, without emotion
"You're going to break his heart"

I could've listened
Would anyone have?

Did I just want to stay with the first person who was good and beautiful?

My Love For You Spans the Concept of Time

What is worse?

Being in a relationship or single?

Relationship
Pro: someone to kill cockroaches
Con: someone to kill

Single
Pro: watching rom-coms
Con: eating alone

Casual sex or solo sex?
Anal sex or no sex?

Speaking Spanish with an American accent
or using vague gestures?

Cockroaches or large spiders?

Getting into a fight with someone before they die
or not speaking to them before they go?

Changing the world inside or outside the system?

Lip fillers or breast implants?
Vegan or free range?
Socks or bare feet?

Kissing with bad breath
or holding a sweaty hand that doesn't fit quite right?

Doing something against your gut feeling
or doing nothing?

Staining your bed with blood or ketchup?

Attaining a certain peace
with hallucinogens
or not doing drugs at all?

Aching for something beautiful
or not having memories that make you yearn?

You Are There, On This Other Plane

The first dream
April of last year

Roses
Photograph
Camera down
Grabbed my hand
We ran
Through a meadow

> *beyond*

I tried to forget
But I haven't forgot
I think I do
And then I dream of you

I want to push this desire away
For if it came near
If you came near
What am I most afraid of?
It going away—
Or knowing it never will?

So I will keep seeing you
In my dreams

You had died
I had said
"I can tell him how I feel now"
I lay on the ground above your body
It was covered in stones
They pressed into my cheekbone
We were closer than we had ever
Been

I Want to Want

My lower back digs into my mattress
The outside of my legs press in to my white sheets
Open
Wide
Ready
To receive
My inner thighs would kiss his bony hip bones

    This morning may have began
    Thinking of a man
    But
    I was feeling so good
    Without one that
    I alchemized
    Transcended
    Into my own desire
    For my desiring

The well, deep & luminous
My wishes surface
And I'm pulling. them. out.

…I notice the space it leaves…
The desire it keeps
Is not a void.

Spoons / All For You

I went camping
For the first time in five years.
Out of my comfort zone
Not camping
But camping with many people
I brought my own food
My own plate, a red rimmed
cartooned one,
Partially melted, a character's
Face fuzzy.

I had food to share, too:
Salsa
Coconut yogurt
Jalapeño cheese puffs
Barbeque mushroom jerky

But one spoon.

So I borrowed four.

Anna made eggs with
Zucchini and feta,
Asked if I wanted some.
"Sure, I'll have a little."
I took a small scoop
Topped it off with salsa,
Then licked the spoon.

I set the spoon down
Took another clean spoon
To dole out on others'
Plates.

I put Elisa's on
Eggs still in the pan
"Am I going to eat them like that?"
She asked.

"No, I was just in salsa
Mode. I'll dish you up."
Oh no. Was my crush on
My friend obvious because I
Put his eggs in a bowl
And not hers?
I fixed her one.

Still hungry, I opened a pint
Of coconut yogurt,
And added it to my plate
With another clean spoon.

The spoon succumbed to a salsa river
On the red plate.

I grabbed another spoon.

"Who would like coconut yogurt?"

Everybody did.

Anna instructed me to set it
In her bowl.

Elisa was searching for a
Clean container
But there were none.
She opened her mouth.

A lump made its way from
The spoon
To her lip
Missed her mouth
Tumbled on her bikinied breast
And plopped on the dirt,
Next to a pinecone.

"I am so sorry!"
For the stain
For the worry of her germs.

She cleaned up.
My friend looked at me,
Sitting on a cooler,
With his alpine lake eyes.

"You're going to put that spoon
Right in my mouth."

And I did.
The spoon went from his mouth to the yogurt,
and to his mouth again.

And then I got another spoon,
Put it in the container,
And gave it to Elisa.

"All for me?"
She asked.

Dreams Divided by Stanzas

Someone was telling me something
Something about sleeping with the clouds
right below.

My boyfriend (very new) made me
A cake and we had a date on a balcony
In an old house in the South
He was wearing a white shirt, maybe a bow tie
And I looked up from the water at us
Bobbing, floating,
thinking, *Wow.*

I was asleep but part of me
Wasn't. I was in a crowd,
Walking, wool jacket,
Hood over my head and half my face
A man held my hand,
We were cherry-picked happy.
He got closer,
Recognized me, and
                    let go.

I was at a cool concept store
and wanted to buy shoes.
I asked if they had any
that were not a thousand dollars
and then I saw you.
We embraced, and still in it,
you said, "You don't need shoes, I will carry you."

You visited me,
Right outside my bedroom window.
You came to say hello,
The stars illuminating your presence.
You might have said something else, too
Maybe telling me a story.
I almost asked, "Do you love me?"
But then I fell asleep,
dreaming.

Spring's Scent

The night smelled like cigarettes
Even though I was inside the bar
It smelled like freshly washed hair
Tequila
Tater tots
And veggie burgers

It smelled like new denim,
My jeans that fit tight
Unwashed
Straight from the sale rack

It smelled like excavated dirt
From a construction site
We walked past

It smelled sexy, potent,
The flowers in bushes, trees,
Stems

It smelled like leather—
The couch comforted me
In the uncertainty

It smelled like salt
His sweat

And then like latex

Because young people
Need to have
More sex

I told myself after I said
I have to wake up early

And Then (And That's When)

Actions over words
And over delivering
And under promising

Yet his words
Are full of love, too
They are fuller, more weighty
Than the simple
Declaration of it

"Promise me you'll never
Do anything that hurts you
To make me feel good."

"What's your favorite pie
From Lovely's?"

"What cute thing
Did you want me to say?"

He hasn't said I love you, but
He says it in his head
I know because his eyes
Dart
Searching my face
For an opening

Instead he takes a big breath
Lets it go

He knows when
I think it
"What?" he asks
With the earnest spirit
That I would tell him

I want to have
Many moments of loving him
Spread out
And also close together
Of in love
And loving
And loved
Before I say it

So I can say,
Yes, of course I love you.
I love you so much.
I loved you then
And then
And then
And then (and that's when)
And then and then
And now
Of course now
  So much now

I Have to Go

The towering golden angel
The sun made her even more gilded,
though it would be beneath the horizon
before the hour was up.

Grant me freedom—I rang the bell.

The late afternoon light illuminated pretty masculine details
like large plants and stone figurines.

"I have a question for you but I don't know if I should ask it."

He looked like a little kid on Christmas morning.
Was it one where you saw Santa's beard fall off,
or one where you could detect a present based on its shape
while the sun was about to rise?

"If you don't want to say it, you can write it down!"

The second.

We stared at each other
mystified to be in this same trance.
I broke it by leaving.

I wrote about that afternoon
before the sun set
with the books
and the mushrooms
and the sake
and the silence
and the wide eyes
and I just want you to know
that I didn't want to leave

You Saw Me First

When I was in the street
Lost

You saw me for the first time
And realized
All the moments before this
You were too

Part II: Need

Power

Can you blame me for being an addict?
When I've been taught to
Internalize the male gaze?
If they give me
    Power,
Then I have some,
Too.

I don't need every man to
    Fall for me
Their lust is not
Accumulated into a bank account.

Using white men's
Attention to make me feel
More valuable when I could've
Cut the middleman
Out and earned
More from the start.

How to Make Time Move Slowly

Walk by the same plant daily
Stare at a blank page
Hold plank pose

Look at someone's face
        And eyes
        And hands
        After saying
I love you

What We Don't See

It is not lost on me
That you gave me
A page of "Blindness"
To read

If you were to know me
Would you stop
Dreaming about me?

I don't know you well
But my heart does

How many opportunities
Will I miss
If I don't believe
I belong in my dreams?

A Wish to Live

"I am alone but not lonely,"
I said in response
To the old man at the café
Who at breakfast announced to his group,
"I'll talk to her, she seems lonely."
He leaned back after I spoke,"Oh."

A woman said, "Oh, that's good."

"I read a variation somewhere," I didn't say.

Later that day
I tried snowshoeing
Around a lake covered
In ice with snow atop

But I simply
Walked in boots, sinking,
Stubborn, and then hypervigilant
Looking for moose, mountain lion
Clapping, making noise

This is how people die, alone
(It was not a death wish
it was a wish to live)
to feel the snow squeak
to sweat with six layers
a numb face full of tears
in this living
I would surely meet someone

An abandoned RV, out of place
The lights off, and then on
I panic and run
on the Nordic tracks

Packed snow made me go faster
Away from danger

I stopped when I could no longer
My breath still labored when
Three young men, with sleds and beers
Came around a bend
They were ahead
Didn't see me,
But I wanted to join

Eventually my presence was known
Their confusion
When I didn't meet them in the parking lot
But stayed in the meadow of snow
Lying down
I popped up to say, "I had to make one last snow angel!"
Lots of nodding.

I walked by their van
Said hello
They asked me questions
We spoke
I asked if they saw a moose
They didn't think moose lived here
I said I saw tracks
No way
I said I have a video
No way no way
Just you wait
The movie played, all ten seconds
Their faces blank
Those are rabbit tracks
Their faces dropped

She's pretty but dumb
Maybe they thought

I left
Drove carefully down the mountain
With fifteen feet of snow and ice
On either side
Upset for feeling so stupid
Don't I know what a moose track looks like?

I could have figured it out
Why couldn't I figure it out?

More / Extra / Read All About It

I've thought about responding
To this message in so many ways.

Funny
Mean
Funny/Mean
Pathetic
Dramatic
With a Question
Or Two
Indifferent
Apathetic
Curious

And all the ways I could say,
"You're going to have to try
Harder than a paragraph.
Maybe a greenhouse of rare orchids
In my apartment or a picnic
In a tree
Or literally, anything else."

But now
I sit here in my bath
Remembering how blissed
Out I was in yours,
And you said, "You're incredible."

And I've been doing fine

And are you just lonely

Refuge in
Not responding

In having power
In not being the one
Waiting for something

And yes, I want you to want me

But what do I want?

Do I want to feel like that?

Heat and Dark

I took a photo
Before I closed it

I want to know how you read the
Letter when it arrived

In the street?
On the stairs?
At your desk?
Did you pour a drink?
Light incense?

Did you read it line by line,
A little afraid?
Did you jump around, searching
For an "I love you"
        "I miss you"
        "I need you"
But they were not there

Do you read it every night
By candlelight
Tempted to burn it
Be done with me once
And for all

Yet the wax seal won't dissolve,
It melts instead

I recite my words
like prayers
Drifting off to sleep

Let Me Out or Let Me Go

I want to be more
Than your muse.
I want to be
Free
With
You

Write a Love Story Without a Partner

Once, in a dance class,
When I was an adult,
The task was to stare at the mirror
Into our faces
For long enough.

I stood and then sat
With my long-sleeved shirt
And stretchy pants

Could my teacher, Montserrat,
See my tears?
I was looking at myself
The way I've looked at men I've fallen for

Curiously, softly, admirably.
With a touch of longing.

Sing

I have nothing left to say
The scar tissue has formed
In my throat
From trying to tell you
So many times

You Wanting My Love
Is Not the Same As You Loving Me

You had somebody to love
I had myself

If I were to be with someone
It wouldn't be to love them
It would be to forget about you
Through them
And who likes being
A ghost?

So did I miss the best part?
Being outside in the orange hue?
Haven't I been looking at everything that way
Anyway?
What things could be
Instead of what they are?

Where will I be
When you're ready for me?
Not here
No more
No longer

Close the Line

Why do I go to bed wondering
Why I didn't open a book?
Why don't I call my grandpa?
Or bake cookies for my neighbors
Or take ten minutes to meditate
Or bring a bag to pick up trash
The birds and their babies pick at
Lying on the veins of
Trees, intermixed with
Fallen flowers
And seeds
It doesn't take much
So what am I doing instead?
Ruminating over why this man isn't
Talking to me

Why do we allow men to bring us down?
Is it so we have an excuse not to be brave?

Walls

It is in the loneliness
In the absence
In the space
In the silence
That I find
seeds solid enough to touch
and ground fertile enough to dig
But the seeds are tiny
And disappear readily
And
The ground grows weeds too

Part III: Grief

White Beads Embroidered as Fiddlehead Ferns

I sold my wedding dress today.

I forgot to thank it.
For making me feel like a woman when I first tried it on
For making me fall in love with me
Like how I wanted to be in love with him

But I still got to wear it

Even though I didn't want to send
    The invitations
Even though I looked in the mirror
    On my wedding day, unrecognizable
Even though I asked him to postpone
    He said no
Even though I wanted to keep my name
    I took his momentarily
Even though I barely wrote my vows

(And writing is like breathing for me)

I still wore it,
I still did it.

Let There Be a Last Time

The first time
I was scared to be with a man
I was 18
he went to MIT
Alone in my dorm room
I was doomed
Where was my roommate?
Why did I invite him into my space?
Why won't anyone barge in?
I stared at the pink Andy Warhol poster by the window. It read,
"The idea of waiting for something makes it more exciting."
I just want to be alone
I just want him to leave
It was my fault for bringing him in here
Didn't I know what he would want from me?
It was my fault

The next time
I was at a party
I fell asleep on the floor
I woke up to someone's mouth on mine
My 11-year-old self wanted him to be my boyfriend
How could he do this to me?
How could I have wanted him?
Eight years before
It was my fault

The next time
second year of college
One of my roommates
was in the kitchen with me
as I made chocolate chip cookies
and ate the dough
"Look! It's like I'm pregnant!" I said, lifting
up my shirt to show PMS bloat.

"Can I touch it?"
"Sure…"
When his hand lingered too long,
fingers outstretched
moving back and forth across my belly button
 I said
"Stop."
He didn't.
Not until I was crouched in the kitchen corner,
on the floor,
What's more?
My hands over my face
After chasing me, he went to his room and shut the door.
It was my fault.

I moved out.
It cost money.
It was my fault.

My boyfriend never confronted him, never said,
"That was wrong, what were you thinking?"
"How dare you"
"Keep your hands off my girl"
"Off any girl"
"But she's my girl!"

The next time
it was because my husband
betrayed me
And I found out
unsure how he would react
to me being privy to this information

Not one man scolded, told him
What he did was wrong

Why can't men tell other men when they are wrong?
Why do women have to?
Because it was my fault

The next time…
The next time…
The next time…
The next time...
There will be no last time
And it will never be my fault
Even when I thought it was

1. I invited him into my room
2. I went to the party
3. I lifted my shirt to show my belly
4. I didn't really love my husband

But it was never my fault
what they did
and what other men didn't do
to me
for me
Why me?

It was not
my fault.

Allowing

I can't expect my family
To fill in the holes—
The ones in my body
Where men have clawed
And burrowed

But would I've allowed
It if
I felt whole from
The start

I Don't Want to Grow Up

The first time I had sex
I existed for
Someone else's pleasure

Suddenly
I was pushed
Rolled
Onto the hardwood
A doll
someone grew tired of playing with

The Drawing in the Museum I Wished I Could Escape Into

Black and white
A woman, alone and naked
Sitting at the edge of a lake
Hair up, looking down
A snow-capped volcano
Reflected on the surface.

My dreams didn't align
With my reality,
So
They didn't make sense.

When we let it all go,
Don't be surprised
What comes up.

There's a reason
Why my body
Gets so sick
After taking
plan B.

Which Is It?

The moment I stopped
Drowning
I started sprinting

I feel like I'm in a daze
Momentum pushes backward,
Spinning

But is it from grief
Or gratitude
That I get to live this life?

A Year of Hope

Is love
The reason for building
and rebuilding lives
Laying the foundation
and burning it down
Is something so revolutionary
Only possible
With somebody else

It's been a year
Of thinking about you
And being a little mean to myself
Every time I do

Am I mad that I
Tried to conceal me
In a manner
Meant for revealing?

Am I tired of believing
Every day that *this
Could be the day*?

I'd betray myself
If I kept hoping.

Records Broken in My Back Seat

You're more than a memory

You're reimagined
Every night
You're there for a moment
Every morning

What's the difference between giving up
And giving it a rest?

Why am I driving so fast
When I missed the exit anyway?

Worlds Within Worlds Within Worlds

I'm sitting in a graveyard
Of trees
I do not know how long
They have been lying here.

Their weight is supported
By the earth
Not by their roots

Resting or dead
Or somewhere else

Perhaps I'm afraid
of getting to the end
Whenever that may be
And discovering all the living
I didn't do

NW 24th and Pettygrove

Why is nobody evacuating?
I crossed the street, wanting to wait
in the middle of it
Knees bent, legs apart
Bracing

I thought I felt an earthquake
But it was the weight of you
Falling off me
I looked around
Did anybody else feel it?
A dad on a skateboard holds
A metal to-go cup
His toddler between his legs with a blue helmet
They smile at me twice

At a Table in East Village at Eighteen

I forced him to say
"I do not love you" 10 times
to erase that he ever did.

My heart cannot be broken,
just cracked open, split wide

*Things that Have Stayed with Me
From People Who Have Not*

"That's what you're doing—what they've done to you. Leave. You left."

"I said to my mom, 'What the fuck are you doing? Ignoring a call? That's your BEST FRIEND!'"

"I just don't think you value my time."

"Promise me you'll always be Sara Sebastian."

"She's a writer!"

"You aren't philosophical enough."

"Don't say that."

"I'm sorry, it's just—you're so beautiful."

"Sarbear."

Wouldn't It Be Easier?

When I thought I was pregnant,
taking test after test only to
Sometimes think, Maybe this would be
Easier to have a life made for me—even
One that meant I was with someone,
A parent with him—but only to wonder if
I were in love with somebody else—
And as time went on, to be sure I was
And to resist it and suffer—but wouldn't
It still be easier—that prescripted life—
Than being free to choose mine in a sea
Of so many overwhelming dreams?

Part IV: Love

We Call So Many Feelings Love

Why does "Love" have to be at the end?
Can't we love now?
Must we go through the other emotions first?

No, love is accessible now
But you've built up things around it
Need
Grief
Desire
Control

So you are going back to the beginning
Ok
Ok
Ok

You can love
You are love
Remembering

Invitation

The thing is
If I were to see you
I would tell you I love you

And then I would have no choice
But to tell you every night

And would that get monotonous for you?

That is how I can justify not telling you

Or rather
Every time I told you
I love you
It would be a limitless, boundless
Invitation

What then?
Well, if the stakes are that high
I must tell you

(Maybe you would not like my love but
 maybe it would change your life)

Expression

She didn't use her body
Only body language
To loosen his grip on the world

Re: Why did I do that?

I can love the part of me
That fell in love
With you.
That's what I have to do.

To Leave It Behind

I woke up early
On January 1st
And gathered my heavy, fluffy duvet
Around me and walked us out
On the porch
To see the sunrise.

It was still dark,
The sun still beneath us.
I could see my breath,
Toes without socks, numb.

Just a few more minutes, time said.
I noticed the clouds changing color,
Ever so slightly, and then,
In an instant akin to an inhale, there the sun was,
Just like us,
Awake and here for another year.

The sun and I, looking at each other,
Made a promise then.
We didn't know what it was,
There were no words.
Two soldiers from opposing sides
face to face just as the
White flag waved.

Witnessing lives
Being renewed
Rebirthed
Able to start again

Where to now?

Goddess

How I'd reach for grapes
Drape them above
Dappled in sun
Mouth whole

What I'd do to sweat
Slippery calves
Rib rising
Heat on my brow

How I would hold a hand
Whose no matter
Palm to palm
Fingers rest

I grant wishes that aren't mine
We idolize gods, but why?

I Want for Nothing

I made pancakes
for someone
who woke up in my bed
          but who I haven't kissed.
I just want to say "I love you, I love you, I love you,"

And let it spill out   of my tongue
but I don't.
Instead I let it come
from my hands

In how I cover the chocolate chips
with batter from my fingers
          so the chocolate doesn't burn,
In how I grip my steering wheel to drive so far to see him,
In how I hold his hands when we dance,
In how I allow mine to be held.
It is enough.

No Such Thing

Thank you to the friends who have saved and deleted
Four phone numbers over the past
Three years

Thank you to the friends who've been a mirror,
Patient in letting me look in, holding me
In moments of awe and pain

Thank you to the friends who've written,
Hosted me, fed me, put flowers next to
My bed

Thank you to the friends who have
Compassionately
Pointed out or outlined
Another perspective
Aka
Called my ass out.

Thank you to the friends
Who've invited me somewhere
To a wedding
To dinner
To their home
To do nothing at all

Thank you to the friends who've sent me recommendations
Wanting to fix my life
But knowing I have to

Thank you to the friends who've
Read my tarot
Read my writing
Read my face
Read between the lines

Who've moved me forward
No time for self-pity, girl
The world is pulsing right here
Like you

Thank you to the friends
Who I admire and never tell
For taking care of themselves
for coordinating their jewelry
For speaking so eloquently
with brevity
freely
And for too long

(For there is no such thing)

Paper Maps

We held each other
Terrified, in a tent
Close to the trail, by the forest
Where earlier,
Women with guns and dogs told us to be careful
—those mountain lions are no joke—
And we looked behind every few steps.

One hundred miles east,
We shared a campground with
Two other parties.
The party of one invited us into his trailer,
And pulled out his gun, unloaded.
"If you're going into mountain lion
Country, you need to be packing."
A retired forest ranger
Gave stories of the big cats I still think about.

& I still think about the horseback riding,
Vanilla milkshakes, digging for fossils,
Hiking in a bright blue basin,
The Painted Hills, the Olympic Mountains,
Foggy views from bridges over rivers,
Tired sunny afternoons searching for
Gasoline, ice, and electrolytes,
And coming back to the city where we lived,
The luggage still on the floor,
And hours, maybe days, in bed
Even after all of that.

Why Now?

My grandpa,
with the purest heart held by the strongest lungs,
can barely speak anymore.

I buy a bonsai tree and place it behind a birthday card
from his brother in North Dakota.
I ask if he wants black licorice, and to keep looking
at me in the eyes if so.
He eats a few pieces and then closes his eyes again.

I find a playlist with music from the 60s and
sit there listening to Do You Believe in Magic, crying,
wondering why I haven't told him all the reasons
I love him until now.

It's Here (It's Time)

Let this be beautiful
I think to the purple lilacs
In the black vase
Next to a beeswax candle
With black soot all around

Honey scented,
The wax and the flowers

I take two minutes
put my toothpaste
Where it belongs
Gathering oils and lotions
Wiping the bathroom counter

I would go to bed
Giving these items I treasure
More opportunity to be
Treasured

I have time to look
Time to refill their water
Time to set their altar

I have time even if I must repeat it

Even if the world makes us believe we don't have any

A Full Moon in July

I'm learning a lot about love lately,
felt it from every direction last night
as a home-made dandelion salve was rubbed on my neck,
as far into the creases of my back it could reach
with the confines of a tank top.
My face warm from the fire,
my ears allowing in guitar, ukulele, other people's voices,
my mouth let the pilsner settle for a moment
before swallowing,
closing my eyes when
he worked on a spot melted from touch.
His knees helped my back straighten.

Later that night, I was given a gift.
I guess I needed someone to ask me
why I can be this here but not that there.

"It's so fascinating how I started filming you on our hike
and you started this minutes-long story
and when I stopped recording you said,
'What are you doing? The story's not over'
and tonight you read a 10-page poem and
you danced ballet to a house-song.
Well, you were a little apprehensive.
But the point is, it's amazing to watch you,
someone so unapologetic, and then to see you piss
all over your writing which means so much to you.
Damn. I wonder where I do that in my life."

I traced my tongue against the back of my teeth.

Later, just before sleep, "Your dancing was beautiful."

Though the moon lit up the tent, I couldn't see his face.

Then goodnight and silence and a pre-dawn bird summoning the sun.

Redemption

I cried instead
A release all the same
Though instead of out
I drew inward
Fetal position
Covers around me
Hands on my face

What is worth putting there?
What colors are worth a brushstroke?
Can I take time to collect
The berries and plants
Where the colors are birthed?

I want to ask questions
About things
I know nothing about

Today
I spun around
And I spun around
And I spun
In the street

I didn't care who was looking
I didn't even look.

Acknowledgments

Thank you to the teachers who taught me to write, and who saw me and my words— especially my eighth-grade English teacher, Jaime Etheredge.

A big thank you to The Tiny Book Course team: Woz Delgado Flint, Tracie Kendziora, and Lindsey Smith.

Thank you to Write Around Portland, PCC Community Education classes, Jeremy Resnick, and Joshua James Amberson for helping me fall in love with writing again.

To the members of Certainly for making my heart feel at home at long-last— and for making me a better writer. I won't forget the magic we made.

Thank you to Nicki Youngsma and Catriona Setliffe for sharing your writing, listening to mine, and for your presence.

To Cali Rose Karstad for your valuable feedback and brilliance.

To Stacey Katlain for showing up without question in the final hours.

Thank you to Hannah Ronningen for your belief in me.

To Chelsea Kane for sharing our dreams and one of your first poems.

Thank you to the Portland poetry community, Slamlandia, Christopher Luna, and Shiaian Price [TheBathTubPoet] for encouragement and inspiration.

Thank you to Valeria Lugo, for so much, and for reading my poems.

To Jim Trumbull for being willing to do whatever it takes.

To Anne Flamio for calling me within seconds after I made the book announcement and for sharing my writing.

Thank you to the nearby forest for providing daily sanctuary.

Thank you to Leilani Rapaport for nurturing my creativity.

Thank you to my friends for providing insight, and for celebrating & loving me.

And to my family for their support and love—my sisters, Sophie, Kristina, and Rach; my brother, Ted, my dad, Randy; and to my mom, Sandra, for letting me write in every corner of the house, leaving a trail of paper and water glasses—and for your praise, critiques, humor, and compassion.

Sara Sebastian writes poetry and creative nonfiction. She has taught English literature, writing, and social studies in the U.S. and Mexico City. She is a middle child of five who is most at home when dancing and exploring. Find her at sarasebastian.co and say hello.